STRONGER
Together
BOOK 1

Walking Through Trauma, PTSD, & Abuse

SHERRI JOST & TINA CLARIN

Clay Bridges
PRESS

Stronger Together
Walking Through Trauma, PTSD, & Abuse
Book 1
Copyright © 2024 by Sherri Jost & Tina Clarin

Published by Clay Bridges Press in Houston, TX
www.ClayBridgesPress.com

ISBN: 978-1-68488-100-0
eISBN: 978-1-68488-101-7

Special Sales: Most Clay Bridges Press titles are available in special quantity discounts. Custom imprinting or excerpting can also be done to fit special needs. Contact Clay Bridges Press at Info@ClayBridgesPress.com

This book is dedicated to our children with *love* always.
Thank you for not giving up.
We are so proud of you!

Upon the shore where waves embrace,
In sands of time, I found my trace.
Through life's journey, both near and far,
Two sets of footprints marked where we are.

But in the trials, when shadows loomed,
One set of prints became entombed.
When troubles surged and spirits pined,
I walked alone, or so I opined.

"Why did you leave me in despair?"
I cried out into the salted air.
In whispered tones, a voice replied,
"My dear child, I've never left your side.

Those solitary steps you see,
Were when I carried you, set you free.
In moments darkest, when hope seemed lost,
My strength upheld you, at great cost.

For in your weakness, my power's revealed,
In every trial, my love is sealed.
Though footprints fade with each retreating tide,
My presence, steadfast, by your side."

So now I walk with newfound grace,
In sands of time, I see the trace.
For every trial, every burden borne,
I know I'm not alone, not forlorn.

In footprints etched upon life's shore,
I find the love I'm searching for.
With each step taken, hand in hand,
I'm guided by love's enduring strand.

THE WRATH OF GOD IS BEING REVEALED
FROM HEAVEN AGAINST ALL THE GODLESSNESS
AND WICKEDNESS OF PEOPLE,
WHO SUPPRESS THE TRUTH BY THEIR WICKEDNESS.

Romans 1:18 (NIV)

When a person experiences PTSD, trauma, and abuse there are so many questions and never enough answers. One may ask herself the following questions.

Why is this happening?

What is the root cause of this horrible situation?

What did I do or didn't do?

How can I cope?

How and when do I move on?

How and when do I accept what has happened to me?

How do I forgive what I could not control?

How and when do I forgive myself?

When will I believe and not just know it wasn't my fault?

Why was I abandoned?

How can I explain what I don't understand?

When will I understand?

How could someone else possibly comprehend and feel the same kind of frustration, anger, resentment, humiliation, regret, sadness, empathy, or aloneness that she has in her heart and head?

The final question always seems to be "Am I the only person in the world who will ever endure the horrific crimes or trauma, PTSD, and abuse?"

The short answer to the final question is no. REMEMBER: we are NEVER ALONE; we are STRONGER TOGETHER! Leaning on God, finding support groups, reaching out to family and friends who would not dare judge and are a safe place—these are good places to be when you are ready to find answers to the other questions. Therapy, counseling, journaling, telling your story, music, taking a drive, and embracing the calamity are other activities to bring closure. Believing and not just knowing you will get past the horrible situation/s, abuse, PTSD, and trauma is a step in the right direction for closure (answers to the questions) as well.

There is a REASON for all that has been endured (even if that reason is not clear, is not known, or is not understood), surrendering to the plan, and knowing you have the power and control to never be in such a situation again. Realizing how STRONG you have become; for yourself, for family, and for your children is one more step for closure.

There have been survivors of such circumstances before you, and there will be survivors after you. YOU ARE A SURVIVOR! Self-care is vital. Self-care can be and should be pursued in different forms such as new goals, new chapters, new adventures, finding an emotional break thru with support books, education, attending or leading support groups to help others, volunteering at a shelter for victims of trauma and abuse, and listening to yourself, to your heart, to your inner conscious, and overcoming the challenge of never giving in, never giving up hope, and never believing you are alone.

After all the above has been completed during your walk-through to healing and self-forgiveness - there is still the ultimate question lingering in the back of one's mind Does anyone ever get closure, completely? Perhaps it depends on how one views closure, and that is only for you to decide. Fair retribution and justice may not always be the same. Yet, those who perpetrate evil, eventually pay for their crimes. That it is not in our control. We need to focus on what we can control and make the decisions to accept happiness, trust in God, trust in those that love us, allow the mind to be at peace, and help move on and forgive.

Recognize that I am able to and very capable of speaking about the abuse, trauma PTSD and be okay; I am able to lead a healthy happy life with possibilities of new relationships and even a life companion or spouse.

Closure does not mean forget the past, the atrocious circumstances. It means that I know that God has control and will allow me my time to process, and there will be a gradual decrease of self-blame and ill-placed responsibility. And it means nightmares will come to an end.

HE WILL COVER YOU WITH HIS FEATHERS, AND UNDER HIS WINGS YOU WILL FIND REFUGE; HIS FAITHFULNESS WILL BE YOUR SHIELD AND RAMPART. YOU WILL NOT FEAR.

PSALM 91:4-6 (NIV)

We are Christian women who realized through true faith in God that no matter how intense our experiences, everything happens for a reason. Leaning on the word of God and praying for God's protection and strength has led to this life-long journey of faith, self-love, self-preservation, and healing.

This book, along with its sequels, contains vital information to guide and support you as you fight your own battles of trauma, abuse, and PTSD. Whether you have lived or are living in an abusive relationship, have a loved one with a mental illness, a child who struggles to self-regulate, childhood trauma that has left you with PTSD, whatever it may be, we are here to walk alongside you. *Stronger Together* reminds us we are not alone in our struggles. God is always present. Sharing stories that sound familiar and ring true for others is an indication that we are not alone in our struggles or the journey for recovery; we are *Stronger Together*.

Our hope is that as we walk through Trauma, PTSD, and abuse in this book and its sequels that you will find some peace and self-love. You will choose to be your own best supporter and positive influence. You will find strength to reflect on your own situation. You will gain an understanding of next steps or even first steps for moving forward with recovery and healing. You will find that you are strong. You are capable. You are beautiful inside and out. You can and will be the change. You are loved.

You are enough!

Table of Contents

THE LORD MAKES FIRM THE STEPS
OF THE ONE WHO DELIGHTS IN HIM;
THOUGH HE MAY STUMBLE,
HE WILL NOT FALL,
FOR THE LORD UPHOLDS HIM WITH HIS HAND.

Psalm 37:23-24 (NIV)

Could you have ever imagined in a million years that you would even be in this spot in the first place? You have so many concerns, so many thoughts, so many unanswered questions. Whether it was one negative experience with significant impact, the many smaller occurrences of verbal, emotional, or physical abuse, or any other experience that damages your well-being or that of a child; the many faces of trauma, PTSD and abuse have presented themselves.

> *Today might be a good day. Yes, I slept – no it didn't help - I still feel tired. I am here aren't I. I am awake. I am alive yet I am not living. I am exhausted! These are just some of the comments I hear from the low roar of conversation of those around me. I understand. I have said the same things to my family and friends and have said so much more. Yet, nothing seems to help, to help me to be better, or for me to feel better. So, I came here not knowing where else to turn or what else to try... seeking some sort of validation that my life is worth living and that what happened to me is an event – just a horrible moment in time (that lasted 18 months) that does not define who I am or who I will be- not now not ever! I have more questions as I listen to their stories – where do I fall within trauma, PTSD abuse? Maybe I am experiencing all three? Is that even a thing? Although I am trying to make sense of this without worrying my parents it is frustrating because I am failing once again. I can see it (the worry and concern) in their*

faces and hear it in their voices. I do what I need to do to make it through routines of my life and be the responsible adult (19-year-old) that I am. I attend college, go to my part-time job when I am supposed to, hang out with my friends and go to parties and sports games. Yet, it feels like I am not really there – what do they call it? – an out of body experience - I suppose that is what I am feeling it is like. Talking to these people here around me helps for a while but not long enough. Where did the me I knew 2 years ago disappear to? Where is the person who believed that she was able to accomplish any goal she set for herself? Where is the person filled with confidence to achieve the dreams she dreamed? When did the person standing here today show up? When did I stop thinking/knowing I was smart, strong, good enough, worthy, competent etc. I want today to be a good day. I want to live. I know I am alive but I want to feel ALIVE! I want to feel more than this limbo of nothing and numbness. I want the ups and downs that are part of life – that show me I am living. I want to wake up thinking/knowing that Today is a Good Day for Great Day!

It's a fine web that is woven for all who live this life of trauma, abuse, and PTSD every day. We wonder how any of us will wake up, live our day, and eventually find a moment of peace, mindful silence, and rest. We pray for our children to be happy, strong, feel loved, and always wanted. We pray for ourselves to be strong; emotionally, mentally, and physically. We pray for ourselves to focus on the good we find within moments throughout our day. We pray these moments are enough to sustain our ability to stand tall and stay strong as we move through life's day to day routines as if nothing is wrong. We desire only the best for everyone.

One day when the child was around two, we both decided after much fighting that it was time to art ways, but I could not leave my baby with him even part-time to be without me in the smoke-filled house, the yelling, the ignorance of the whole family. No, I could not have that for my baby. I wanted so desperately to stay with my mom even though her mental and physical health was not that great since we lost my dad, who had been her life, her rock, her everything. My husband and mom never got along. It was hell without my child. No way out. Wow! What kind of mom am I? How could this happen? I did not know? I had to do the unthinkable.... Even though my ex and I split, I went over and groveled to come back and live with him again because I could not leave my baby alone with him. As a parent, it is so hard to ever let your babies go, especially in this situation. I knew what I was going back into. I knew it meant more neglect, abuse, and feeling like I was sentenced to a life-time in prison without parole. I didn't commit a crime yet I was punished to the fullest extent of abuse my ex-husband could dole out.

Thank God for my parents sending me to the Catholic school. Thank God for my mom taking me to church because otherwise I would not even know about God. Sure, I was raised and believe there is a God and that He will not forsake the Bible. He will always hold on to His children if you just cry out and ask. God and I found one another again. I called out to God to please help. Please get me out; I am so scared and so miserable. I am so sorry for all I did. Please help me. I want out! I still did not know if He was hearing me or even cared, but I knew deep down He was my only hope. My only constant.

Parents and other caregivers can see so many struggles: so much frustration, confusion, rage, fear, and loss when there is a mental illness present in a child. You know deep down that this is not all your children's fault. They will not diagnose your child/ren the correct way because they have put down on a piece of paper that your child has a mental illness that cannot be controlled. Is there even any hope?

Finally, you have your other child back to a point where life seems bearable once again. Sure, you still have to deal with the verbal and physical abuse, but you overlook that because it is not happening as much. Your child is not screaming and yelling every night. It is like, at last, after all this time, your child has come back to you. You take what you can get at this point because you know how much worse it could be. It is so scary that you do not know which way to turn, which doctor is going to help, or who is even willing to give you the time of day because you have been on this roller coaster for so long. You increase your speed climbing up the hill only to be followed by accelerating downhill just as fast and at what cost. You feel such loss, fear, and frustration, knowing that all the hard work that you thought finally had started paying off was a waste.

The problem is deep down you know there is a part that cannot control this because of the mental illness. The hell will not let up, the torment does not take a vacation, and the bitterness and resentment cannot be destroyed no matter what tools you may use. You feel the emptiness inside when you know that you are on your last fiber of stability. You know that you can't take anymore.

> *It is very hard to pray for nine years and not know if I would even live long enough to see the result of all those prayers. I don't even know if God ever heard me or is going to get me out. Why did He allow me to be here in the first place? I ask what I did to have this happen and how to get out. There are so many questions, and when you are that miserable, you wonder if He even cares. Ok, where is He now, then? How much more of the beatdown could He allow me to take? I thought I was a pretty good person. I took care of me and my babies, I tried to be a good daughter, a friend, a granddaughter, sister, niece. etc. I went to church, and school, did confession, and was raised in a good home. You know you have hit your lowest point when you sit and beg for some guidance because you have lost all sense of hope and tell your kids they have the control to do whatever they want. That is when you know it is time; you pray and pray for some miracle.*

I am your mother, my abusive and now decimated marriage, is not your fault. Yet you have been negatively affected more than I know. I am sorry it took so long to remove us from the horrors of the situation and find a way to get us back to living and not just surviving. I want to take you and hold tight without ever letting go. Pour my love and soul into you to breathe new life and save you from the demons in the shadows of your mind. I, as your parent, want you to live life to the fullest, even with all the ups and downs that life will be guaranteed to throw your way. No matter the situation, the glass can be half-full or half-empty this perspective does and will continue to matter and determine the outlook on the days ahead. You and I are stronger together, we are stronger than we know, and we will survive and move forward by the Grace of God. Our Belief in God is our mainstay for sanity and testament to living one day at a time the best we know how. Our Faith in the Lord Jesus Christ through desperate prayers help us live our lives through the challenges we now face because of the abuse endured, the trauma ensued, and the PTSD yet to be defined.

What can be done to help this child, as the self-destructive behavior, angry tantrums, anxiety and paranoia are getting worse. This child has constant fear, anxiety, rage, resentment, and questions. Yet, they are so scared they bury everything and ignore everyone. The daily routine of survival becomes the norm for the child just to make it through the day. Unfortunately, this may include treating a parent like a punching bag even when that person is the constant champion for a better reality.

Questions begin bombarding your thoughts.

> How will you ever be able to help them?
>
> Who is going to advise you on how to help?
>
> Should a diagnosis be sought?
>
> Does the situation warrant hospitalization?
>
> What about child therapy and parental counseling?
>
> What about medications and possible side effects?
>
> Will there be a treatment plan and behavior modification as well?
>
> Can I start a conversation with my child and both of us remain calm and sane?
>
> Can I survive feeling emotionally and physically drained one more time from another out-of-control shouting match episode?
>
> Will this ever end?

He was there in the beginning, and He will be there in the end. When you finally realize He is the one, the alpha and omega, you realize He is the only constant you have. So, you ask yourself why He did do this to you.

> *What did you do or not do that was so horrible in life to justify all of this?*

What did your beautiful babies do? They are so innocent and precious.

Why would God allow them to have to go through this?

Why would God allow this to happen to me?

WHY WAS I FORGOTTEN?

You were supposed to be protected no matter what, and yet you will always believe deep down and say on the surface God will never leave.

Yes, eventually there is light and hope for an end to the chaos and insanity. Ultimately, with a proper diagnosis and appropriate medication we can have open communication with our child. This allows us to move forward with understanding the perspectives of all; those of us entrenched in the situation as well as those of family and friends who watch, wait, and want to help without a true understanding of how.

Reflection

Three ways I relate to this chapter

1. _____
_____
_____
_____
_____

2. _____
_____
_____
_____
_____

3. _____
_____
_____
_____
_____

If I am honest with myself – this is my situation:

_____

_____

_____

_____

_____

_____

_____

_____

_____

_____

_____

_____

_____

_____

_____

_____

_____

_____

_____

_____

My situation (trauma, PTSD, abuse) is
negatively impacting my life in the following way/s:

_____

_____

_____

_____

_____

_____

_____

_____

_____

_____

_____

_____

_____

_____

_____

_____

_____

_____

_____

_____

To move on to a healthy recovery I need to:

_____

_____

_____

_____

_____

_____

_____

_____

_____

_____

_____

_____

_____

_____

_____

_____

_____

_____

_____

_____

_____

_____

_____

_____

Steps/goals to help move forward

1. _____

_____

_____

_____

_____

_____

_____

2. _____

_____

_____

_____

_____

_____

_____

3. _____

_____

_____

_____

_____

_____

_____

Three positive thoughts to focus on before I fall I asleep

1. _____

_____

_____

_____

_____

_____

_____

2. _____

_____

_____

_____

_____

_____

_____

3. _____

_____

_____

_____

_____

_____

Am I waking up in the morning ready to take on the day?

_____

_____

_____

_____

_____

_____

_____

_____

_____

_____

_____

_____

_____

_____

_____

_____

_____

_____

_____

Helpful Resources

The Mayo Clinic
https://www.mayoclinic.org
Mental illness in children: Know the signs

The National Traumatic Stress Network
https://www.nctsn.org
The National Traumatic Stress Network-Creating, Supporting,
and Sustaining Trauma-Informed Care

Child Abuse and Neglect Hotline
1 800-392-3738

Find Treatment.gov
https://findtreatment.gov/what-to-expect/mental-health

Chapter 2
Parent Perspective

CALL TO ME AND I WILL ANSWER YOU,
AND WILL TELL YOU GREAT AND HIDDEN THINGS
THAT YOU HAVE NOT KNOWN.

Jeremiah 33:3 (ESV)

I t feels as if there is no hope in sight except prayer and trusting that God. HE will take care of those sweet innocent babies as He promised. The days and nights struggle on! You are depleted, helpless, and cannot move another muscle. But you have no choice because there is no one else. As a parent, you do not understand why it is so hard to find compassion, a reason, a diagnosis, an answer for what is going on inside of your children. You followed the guidelines, the rules, and the sheet on how to help your child. You paid attention to the signs you were told to look for. You used the strategies you were told to use. Now what? It's all on you (the parent/caregiver), to guide, listen, and try your best not to lose your mind along with your temper, all while trying to remind yourself it's not your child's fault. Yet you don't know for sure if the behavior is because of not enough attention, or even too much attention. Then again perhaps it is a lack of understanding, listening, compassion (on your part) or just a misguided perception (from the child's perspective) that there is a lack of these things.

As your child gets older, they begin to understand how to play the system and manipulate people as well, and this leads you to question your child's motives and feelings that are slowly surfacing from way down below. Is your child remaining calm on the inside or is everything bubbling to the surface? These are all valid questions, and God knows we wished we all had the answers so we could remove ourselves from the situation and this could end.

The logical part of the brain "tells" you that you are rejuvenated and capable. Believing you can do his, you take on the world of your kids, yourself, and any other barrier. Mental health is your everyday life in your home, at work, and in society. Therefore, why is this so hard? Why do you have to deal with all the worry, stress, and various meltdowns on so many levels? Why God?

I was raised by two amazing parents. My dad worked and my mom stayed home. That is how it was back then. I wish it was still that way. I miss my childhood. They played the song "A Baby Changes Everything" at church last weekend for Christmas. It is true. Your life is never the same after having children, and sometimes it's not going to look like the white picket fence with a backyard, dog, and your kids playing with Dad. One day you wake up and ask yourself how you got here and why you chose someone who was the opposite of your dad? The answer is I don't know. The only thing I can think of is he drew me out of my shell. He acted as if he loved me and manipulated himself into my life. I felt bad for him and where he came from. Who knows why we do what we do? Looking back, I did make it. I have no idea except by God's hand how I withstood the situation, the torture, and the abuse for so long. I mean, you cut off your family, your friends, your entire existence for someone who does not care about you. You reduce yourself to abuse, to jail, to neglect, to living in poverty with infestations of bugs and rodents. All for what? For him? After all that, you have a beautiful baby, your life, your everything. This innocent child does not deserve all this, but what can you do now? You have no job because you have no one to watch her. You have no money; he has even stolen your opportunity to get out and have a life. You do the only thing you know how to do: be a mother. You continue to take that fur baby for walks and love her. You take the car when you can, and you go out to the nice suburbs you grew up in where it is clean and the air is fresh. You miss it so much you ache for it. It is so hard knowing you don't live there, and you must go back home to hell. You just want to take the baby and the dog and run far away. Those loves of your life are already so victimized and have so many scars. You have no idea which way to turn, but you must find an outlet. You have your God time, your workout, running, driving, and any therapy you can get. You take time with friends if you have any, but he mostly took that from you. He left you in an abyss, drowning.

Social events (birthdays, holidays, graduations, baptisms, etc.) with family and friends are not easy. You love your family yet family is complicated and get togethers can be overwhelming. You and your child fight very hard to control the emotional rollercoaster the seems to emerge during stressful events. The underlying turmoil caused by an abusive situation creates a gap despite the many challenging conversations with family and the lack of listening and understanding you receive. Therefore, wishful thinking sets in when out at a family event. We long to believe we could just leave early because we weren't feeling good, we were tired, we just needed a break, or we were here for a while – just long enough to be noticed for appearances sake.

PARENT PERSPECTIVE

Experience has taught us that extended family members do not truly understand what you are going through and can only surround themselves with so much of what family and friends see as a toxic environment. That is what we as parents want to say – you truly do not understand what is going on or what we are going through! However, this cannot be said it will burn bridges and you need your family now and you need them later too. So, you sit quiet with your wishful thinking because it's your mom's birthday, it's a holiday party, it's Christmas, it's a wedding, or you are just visiting at a friend's house. The real test is when you decide everything will be fine you and the kid(s) go to dinner at the house the of person you have been dating and sure enough it was going fine until it wasn't. Now, you are feeling judged by the dinner host and just know you will never see them again. You are struggling with you own feelings about this situation, your child and the event unfolding in front you. To your dinner host it appears to be an out of the blue occurrence and unnecessary. While you know this is not the case you are still baffled and embarrassed as you cannot pinpoint what triggered the current explosion and outbursts by your child. You can see your host's thoughts in their eyes and body language - you are seen as the reason for the outburst because you have done or not done something to allow such unseemly behavior. Perhaps out of ignorance (yet not excusable) many hurtful things are said toward both you and your kid(s). You try your best not to say a word because you know that they cannot possibly even remotely comprehend the totality of the situation with such a lack of knowledge on the subject! Not that you didn't try to help them understand in the oh so many conversations leading up to this night.

The question you continue to ask is when that person is going to bail? When will it be too much? How are they going to look at me in the end? At my kids? Are they going to feel sympathy for me, yet talk about me behind closed doors? You just know as much as you want another person in your life, it is not going to happen. However, you want to believe with the right person, it can. God will show you; the problem is, when, when will He show you, it is okay to live your life as a person and not just a mom of kids that need so much mental health care. It's not your fault; it is the struggle of finding balance. You are learning to be ok with how it is and not doubting or asking for confidence. The question that weighs on you is how you can expect someone to come in and love you so much that they want to stay because you don't even know how you stay. You stay because this is your life, your child/ren, and this is the way it is. Now, you know you will never leave your situation because you are the only constant in your children's lives. You are their rock.

The worst part is that at some point you have the opportunity to vent and talk with people, and they listen, trying not to judge and feeling sympathy. Then it hits them, and you can see the embarrassed look and yet astonishment on their faces. And in a split second there is different look as their face changes to sympathy and sadness and the words come out that you do not want to hear. "I have no idea how you do it. I could not do it. I am so sorry." Tears immediately start to run down your cheeks because you feel the sense of hopelessness set in. The most powerful and negative words that anyone could ever say to you are truly spoken. You know that in the end you are on your own and even a therapist has no idea how to help you and your child get the best care possible.

You are left feeling horrible and stuck with the thought that you can't take your child anywhere. You are so frustrated and tired of this. You long for relief, compassion from others, a family that understands, but these never seem to ever truly come?

Then, in a moment of solitude and unexpected "free time" you look at Facebook and see a post about a relative, friend, or child who passed away too soon, received a medical diagnosis, committed suicide, or had an accident. They lost a person, a job, or a feeling of hope and are now buried under the weight of the world. This makes you look at your life. You are still here. Your kids are alive. They are healthy and strong: cognitively and physically okay. Perhaps they are emotionally unstable, but otherwise okay. You feel like crap for even complaining knowing that because of God, you, will make it. You do not know the word DEFEAT!!!! This is the hand you are dealt, and you do your best. You have so much despite feeling miserable and all that you have to complain about. You are blessed and loved,

That is when you lean on the hope and mercy of God because, let's face it, who else do you have? Please help, God. I know you are there and have helped so much already. You wake me up every morning, allow me to work, to have family, to have friends, to have shelter, running water, a church, a life. I am stronger.

Reflection

Three ways I relate to this chapter

1. _____
   _____
   _____
   _____
   _____

2. _____
   _____
   _____
   _____
   _____

3. _____
   _____
   _____
   _____
   _____

How am I taking care of myself physically?

_____

_____

_____

_____

_____

_____

_____

_____

_____

How am I taking care of myself physically?

_____

_____

_____

_____

_____

_____

_____

_____

_____

Am I stressed out by matters that are not in my control?

_____

_____

_____

_____

_____

_____

_____

_____

_____

_____

_____

_____

_____

_____

_____

_____

_____

_____

_____

_____

_____

To move on to a healthy recovery I need to continue

_____

_____

_____

_____

_____

_____

_____

_____

_____

_____

_____

_____

_____

_____

_____

_____

_____

_____

_____

_____

Steps/goals to help move forward
(different from previous response/s)

1. _____

_____

_____

_____

_____

_____

_____

2. _____

_____

_____

_____

_____

_____

_____

3. _____

_____

_____

_____

_____

_____

Three positive thoughts to focus on before I fall I asleep
(different from previous response/s)

1. _____

_____

_____

_____

_____

_____

_____

2. _____

_____

_____

_____

_____

_____

_____

3. _____

_____

_____

_____

_____

_____

What am I doing to wake up in the morning
ready to take on the day?

_____

_____

_____

_____

_____

_____

_____

_____

_____

_____

_____

_____

_____

_____

_____

_____

_____

_____

_____

Helpful Resources

The National Child Traumatic Stress Network
https://www.nctsn.org/

Child Mind Institute's
https://childmind.org/
Child Mind Institute's Helping Children Cope After
a Traumatic Event: A recovery guide for parents, teachers,
and community leaders

Child Abuse and Neglect Hotline
1 800- 392- 3738

Domestic Shelters.org
www.DomesticShelters.org
Protecting your children in the court system

National Domestic Violence Hotline
1- 800- 799- 7233

IN THE WORLD YOU WILL HAVE TRIBULATION.
BUT TAKE HEART;
I HAVE OVERCOME THE WORLD.

John 16:33b (ESV)

Okay, here we go, mom is taking me to yet another doctor to perform tests and advise meds, yet nothing seems to be working. I still don't have a clue as to what is wrong with me or how to treat it. I feel like a guinea pig. The doctors just try out things and tell my mom to do this or that and try a another/different medication. I am tired of try this try that – oh it didn't work – okay let's do it all over again with something else. I know my mom worries about my meltdowns, my raging temper, blackouts, and self-harm. She is doing the best she can. The flashbacks seem to be the root cause but what do I know I am not a doctor. I wonder if anyone listens to my mom. I know they are not listening to me.

I love to see my family and get together for birthdays, holidays, graduations, etc. So much fun and yet the world seems to come crashing down on me. I can feel the rage rising and I know I won't be in control when it is unleashed. Why is this happening (again), what's wrong with me? I don't like the looks I am getting from my grandma and others; I don't like the way they whisper about me as I walk away. It feels as though people are against me, that I must always apologize even if I did not do anything wrong. When I get home, I cry in despair or lash out at mom because it is easier to be mad at her than figure out what is wrong with me and how to "fix" it.

I can't remember a time when my life was normal (like my friends). I think back to the park, doctor visits, grocery shopping, and the million other daily routine items that parents do with their children. I only see my mom in those memories – my dad never did anything like that he was never around and if he was, he was usually in a bad maybe even a mean mood. When I was little, I loved my dad and I wanted his attention. I wanted him to like me enough to come visit me and keep his promises. I did not understand why he didn't like me, why he never came to visit and why he broke his promises. My mom talks about her dad and how he was her rock. My grandpa was there for my mom a positive part of her life, involved and engaged, loving and caring. I wish I had a dad like that but I was not so lucky.

Mom told me that the next step was to see a psychiatrist and a therapist. I needed to talk to someone about my feelings and my nightmares. I told them about when I was younger and I would see how strangers look at me with the eyes saying "what the hell are you doing? And then they look at my mom with eyes that say "Can't you get your kid under control?" I told these people how I overheard my mom speaking with grandma about how sad she is and angry at the same time that the parents look at her and she just knows that they are thinking "I don't want my kid hanging around with all that crap and crazy behaviors, poor kid and poor mom but my child cannot learn anything good from that situation - That parent has no control, the kid is messed up. The family is very questionable." I told them how she cried as she told my grandma that she was at the end of her rope she had reached a breaking point - she did not know what to do. Do *we move? Do we try a different school? Look for new friends? Should she try meeting someone (again) for herself and to bring in to the family dynamic? Maybe it will help to have that other disciplinary person in our lives. This stuff didn't seem to interest the people I was talking to. So, I spoke with these people some more, told them my stories, my nightmares and dreams. I told them about the vague pictures in my head like memories yet not sure if they were real. Now, mom is telling me that my dad should be in jail for things he did to me and my sister and the many ways he hurt us. However, the law is not on my side. Apparently, there is a time line on bad things that bad people do and after that time has passed those bad things are no longer bad enough for the law to step in and try to make it right.*

I realize I am never home anymore. I want my own life, I want to live a normal life, and although I am still struggling, I am trying to get the ruins of my life put back together. It is better this way, alone and never home because I don't fight with my mom as much. I wish I could stay calm when I talk to my mom. I wish I could talk with my mom more I know we could figure this out together with less challenges. I know she wants, so badly, to help me succeed and be the best version of myself. I want this too. How do I get there, how do we get there?

I do not have the answers nor do I know where to begin this next step to being and having a healthy mental state. I know my mom and I have already sacrificed so much of our lives. We have already faced so many demons, fallen through so many tunnels of despair, and found the lowest point of our existence, and yet she says with faith and conviction that we have arrived on the other side by the grace of God.

I know that I can never go back to that lowest point again! The path is not clear, there is no guarantee, and I am sure there is no easy outcome. I know through all the drama, the struggles, the roller coaster of emotional battle grounds, the physical fatigue, and the lack of understanding, there is forgiveness. I know this, because there are times when I wake up the next morning, with a sense of hope, refreshment, empathy, and compassion. I know that beginning a day with such thoughts is a good day to have a good day! I want to hug my mom (I can't even remember the last time I did that).

Reflection

Three ways I relate to this chapter

1. _____

_____

_____

_____

_____

2. _____

_____

_____

_____

_____

3. _____

_____

_____

_____

_____

How can I put the best effort into my relationships?

_____

_____

_____

_____

_____

_____

_____

_____

_____

_____

_____

_____

_____

_____

_____

_____

_____

_____

_____

_____

_____

_____

How did I make someone smile today?

_____

_____

_____

_____

_____

_____

_____

_____

_____

_____

_____

_____

_____

_____

_____

_____

_____

_____

_____

A quote by Zig Ziglar "Remember that failure is an event, not a person."
How does this make a positive impact my life and decisions?

_____

_____

_____

_____

_____

_____

_____

_____

_____

_____

_____

_____

_____

_____

_____

_____

_____

_____

_____

_____

_____

_____

Steps/goals to help move forward
(different from previous response/s)

1. _____

_____

_____

_____

_____

_____

_____

2. _____

_____

_____

_____

_____

_____

_____

3. _____

_____

_____

_____

_____

_____

Helpful Resources

Cadey
Perspective-Taking in Childhood: Definition and Resources Cadey
https://cadey.co › articles › perspective-taking

Wonders Counseling
Resources for Child Centered and Directive Play Therapy in ...
https://wonderscounseling.com/resources-helping-children-anxiety-
play-therapy/

Sammantha Snoden (Book)
Anger Management Workbook for Kids: 50 Fun Activities to Help
Children Stay Calm and Make Better Choices When They Feel Mad by
Samantha Snowden MA

Vanessa Green Allen, M.ED. (Book)
Me and My Feelings: A Kids' Guide to Understanding and Expressing
Themselves Paperback
by NBCT Vanessa Green Allen, M.Ed.

Jenna Bernam (Book)
The Self-Regulation Workbook for Kids: CBT Exercises and Coping
Strategies to Help Children Handle Anxiety, Stress, and Other Strong
Emotions by Jenna Berman

Chapter 4
Identify Coping Skills

BE STRONG AND COURAGEOUS.
DO NOT FEAR OR BE IN DREAD OF THEM,
FOR IT IS THE LORD YOUR GOD WHO GOES WITH YOU.
HE WILL NOT LEAVE YOU OR FORSAKE YOU.

Deuteronomy 31:6 (ESV)

Understanding the process for learning and utilizing coping skills has as many pathways as there are people involved. Coping skills have many levels and while similar in the beginning become very personalized due to the differing perspectives of the child and their caregivers. It is hard for every person to find peace that can keep the path straight and narrow. The forest of lies will manipulate and give so many choices for what to do, how to think, and where to go. The vines and branches will snuggle you tight and make you feel wanted, but they are also keeping your child from expressing and experiencing all life has to offer.

I know I have been judged by people who say they are friends by family and definitely by strangers. I know I have judged friends, family and strangers too. We all judge, but some of us try silently to keep that judgment in our heads, in our thoughts and to ourselves before not having any control of our filters. Children learn to have filters unless there was trauma, PTSD, abuse etc. that changes the neurodevelopment and filters are not created. Wha as seen as outbursts or harsh commentary is actually the absence of filters and how to help change this has not yet been fully discovered. So, the doctors just want to jack around with the meds. They want to increase, decrease, or treat your child as another pawn. You get a different answer every time you go. Every time you know you are setting foot in the office; you are leaving to go to the pharmacy to get

> *more medication. You thank God at that point for the damn government because they cover everything. So many people struggle daily to pay for healthcare; they are loaded down with medical bills with no way out, and their child is worse off than your child. You just thank God for the blessings at that point. Then more thoughts creep in – how are we going to cope with any of this – the change in meds, the behavior and mood changes because of the meds, the highs/ lows caused by trying to balance the dosage of the meds etc. etc. etc. I think to myself – I have no clue I am exhausted and burnt out, I cannot take one more step or move one more inch let alone stay positive. And yet somehow, I find the strength and find myself moving forward to ensure the health and well-being of my children and myself. I am taking it one day at time, one breath at time when necessary, and even one thought at a time.*

Providing support to a child so they will feel love, light and hope takes on many forms as well. The child seeks attention positive or negative to fill the voids of loss and hopelessness. Caregivers respond by engaging in conversations which may be calm and collected or perhaps even an unwanted shouting match. Leaving both sides emotionally and physically drained. In moments like these coping skills can include, active listening (allow the child to vent), walking a way for a few minutes before responding, telling your child during a calm moment I Love You and I am here to help, or a technique to redirect/distract is American Sign Language (ASL).

Every day is new and must be approached with wisdom, grace, and love. This, of course, is easier said than done. Who has this much control over their lives? I must be logical and ready to face the new challenge that is happening at any moment. It's easy to go inside of my head to my safe place, the place no one else can touch, and everyone wants to embrace the fact that I will overcome. It's bac k to reality; the kids are up. What will the day hold? I tell myself to enjoy each moment with my children; smother them with God's love as well as my (momma's) love. It sounds like a no-brainer and completely natural.

Coping Skills can be learned at the therapist's office, practiced in a session and implemented in a moment that requires both you and your child to return to a state of calm and mindfulness. Being intentional with comments and actions to increase the calm and deescalate the feelings that overwhelmed the situation and brought to a boil or even and explosion.

That is what we all hold on to even if just for that moment. A moment when coping skills make a difference and a positive impact on the situation for all involved. You are also hoping, praying, and trusting, in God; and that is what will get you through. Your trust in God to send some magic, a glimmer of realization that you are not alone and you no longer feel alone!

Growing your network of support people and groups is also a coping skill. Managing your Self-Care treatment plan or daily routine to mitigate struggles and episode triggers is vital to improving and increasing your tool box of coping skills. Remain positive and supportive and avoid saying things that minimize one's feelings (Ryder, 2021).

Healing from trauma is possible. Learning how to heal from trauma is an invaluable coping mechanism. "Trauma-focused psychotherapy is one of the most effective things you can do for recovery" (Ryder, 2022).

Reflection

Three ways I relate to this chapter

1. _____

_____

_____

_____

_____

2. _____

_____

_____

_____

_____

3. _____

_____

_____

_____

_____

If I am honest with myself – this is my situation

_____

_____

_____

_____

_____

_____

_____

_____

_____

_____

_____

_____

_____

_____

_____

_____

_____

_____

_____

_____

_____

My situation (trauma, PTSD, abuse) is negatively impacting
my life in the following way/s

_____

_____

_____

_____

_____

_____

_____

_____

_____

_____

_____

_____

_____

_____

_____

_____

_____

_____

_____

_____

_____

To move on to a healthy recovery I need to

_____

_____

_____

_____

_____

_____

_____

_____

_____

_____

_____

_____

_____

_____

_____

_____

_____

_____

_____

Steps/goals to help move forward
(different from previous response/s)

1. _____

_____

_____

_____

_____

_____

_____

2. _____

_____

_____

_____

_____

_____

_____

3. _____

_____

_____

_____

_____

_____

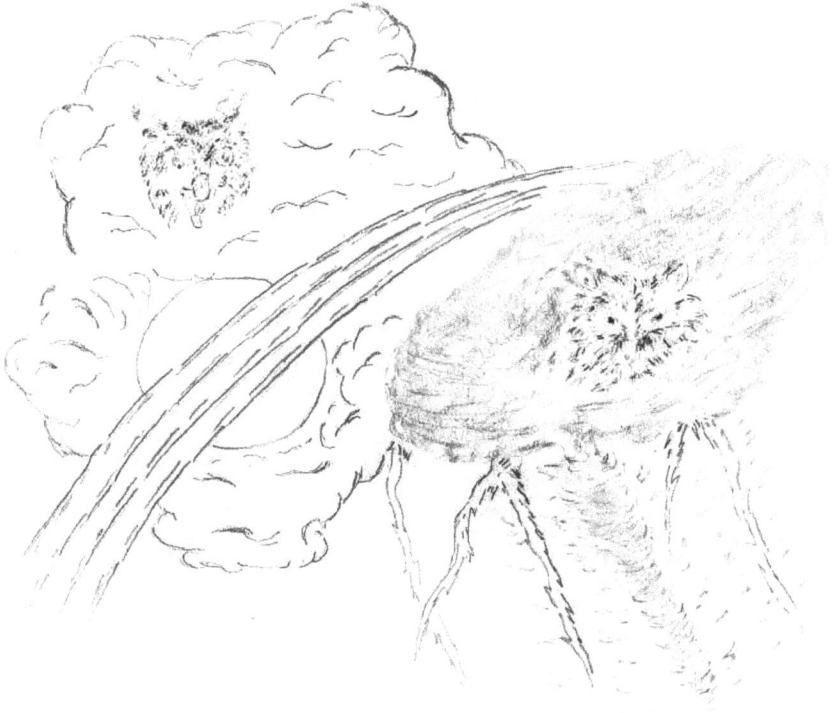

Helpful Resources

Focus on the Family
https://www.focusonthefamily.com/

National Institue of Mental Health
https://www.nimh.nih.gov/health/topics/caring-for-your-mental-health

Tell Med
https://tellmed.org/2020/05/04/build-your-coping-skills-toolbox-
relocate-relax-reframe-recenter-redirect/

Dr. Becky Bailey
I Love You Rituals by Dr. Becky Bailey.
https://www.christianbook.com/

Chapter 5
Walk the Talk

LISTEN TO ADVICE AND ACCEPT INSTRUCTION,
THAT YOU MAY GAIN WISDOM IN THE FUTURE.

Proverbs 19:20 (ESV)

Trying therapy, reading articles for more information, searching the Internet for sources to assist in doing better and being better are some of the options available. These options are for both the adult and child/ren learning to survive and thrive in spite of experiencing Trauma, PTSD, or abuse.

I am 22 years old now and graduating from college soon. I was worried I might not make it to this celebration and passage in life. I was riddle with mental health issues when I entered college, I changed universities twice. I stayed in touch with only a handful of people/friends from high school so that I wouldn't be reminded of the events that led up to an unsettling series of bad choices my freshman year in college. My junior year wasn't much better - I was burdened with Insomnia caused by nightmares from my senior year of high school. Every time I closed my eyes, I saw a face and events that I worked so hard to forget. I couldn't concentrate on school work so I read romance novels 500 +pages a night start to finish. Went to morning classes for 3 hours and came home and collapsed so exhausted I slept without fear of dreaming for 3-4 hours. Woke up with enough energy to go to classes for the next 4 hours and do it all over again. I was too busy to find someone to talk to, too scared that talking would bring back even more memories I didn't want to remember and too focused on my grades and earning my double major with a minor to care that the last 90s days were hazy and recollection of 6 years ago was easier. However, something had to change and soon. I found some solace in instrumental music, chiropractic care, and massage therapy. I could sleep if I listened to the music and it helps changed the nightmares to positive images and happier dreams. The other strategies helped with migraines and relaxation so that sleep was again possible.

Until one or more of these options are making the positive changes needed it is easy to want to escape reality. If you can find the time, you try and find that place of relaxation, patience, understanding, and forgiveness by doing one or more of the following; lie down and rest, take a walk, or go for a drive. Some of this helps some of the time. None of it helps all of the time. Therefore, going to the oh so many, many doctors over the years to find help has led to developing a love/hate relationship with them. You can see your child fighting with every ounce of strength to find him or herself again, to find the family, the friends, the feelings, the love that once was. The darkness or dark spirit seemed to take away the essence of your child so quickly and leave a huge mess full of emptiness and regret. You can see it her eyes that she feels like she is no longer who she once was. Yet, everyone (all the professionals you have seen) is out of answers.

You know your child is still inside there somewhere, but they are fighting all the hurt, all the abusive words and actions, to fight the monster within created by abuse and trauma, and yet still she is fighting to succeed. Sorting out all the feelings of the world around her and from within. Trying to find what is missing, to find the way home (a safe and loving place).

Your heart is breaking as you watch your child struggle and fight. You want to protect her and always be there her. To love and forgive. To hold her and cry with her. However, this is not possible, not now in this moment as she continues to test everything in her chaotic world. The problem is you feel defeated. Knocked down yet again by the inability to successfully help in her time of need, Not to mention every time you take two steps forward, you find yourself deflated and right back at the beginning with no end in sight. If this is how you feel, imagine the feelings your child is experiencing. No wonder it feels like a lifetime of trials and tribulations have been obstructing the path of better days, happiness, and positive thinking.

The days pass quickly and yet feel like slow motion as you are bombarded with the normal mood swings of a teenager that have been amplified by abuse and trauma.

I keep thinking the kids are good. We moved, switched schools, and away from Sperm Donor. Everything will be good. It started rough as I knew it would, but then suddenly it gets easier, a little be better every day. We all get into our routines. I am the happiest of our family of three to have made the move and I do what I can for the girls I always have, and I always will. They are my life. I know no matter what I feel, say, or circumstances live with day and night, I would not trade my kids for the world. Deep down I also know this is not their fault. There are times when I wonder if recent behavior is my child acting out or is this the child's inner voice saying, "I don't know how to do this anymore, Mom. How do I cope with everything that is going on in life and still be able to function in life, society, at home, with people? I am sorry. I will be back. I love you." Then I turn around and BAM! Here is the new you (personality/mood) taking over the old you. This is the one I dread, the one that frustrates me, the one that does not care or that does not love, does not help, the one that always complains and is defiant no matter what I say or do. So now I know the time has come, and I know that I am ing home to pack her bags to go back to the hospital. I am so upset knowing she should not have to keep going back without any hope of getting a diagnosis/treatment plan. Which, of course, is the answer to my prayers. I let the rest of the weekend play its course, and then I face the inevitable – to the hospital we go for a 5150 admit code (72-hour psychiatric hold) and a possible 5250 code [14-day extension of the original 72-hours (Geller, 2006).]

I must be strong and find a way out. Should I start to establish a new life? Should I put down some roots and fight? How do I keep my kids and keep them safe? So many questions.

So, I decided. We are going to church and putting down roots I cannot go underground and leave everyone and everything I know to start a whole new life. I must help my kids, fight back, trust, love, and connect. Each situation is different, and each strategy is not the same; you must do what is best for you and your family to do. You can get all the support and counseling along the way, but it boils down to you and your family. Each dynamic, each person, each opinion, and thoughts are all different, and everyone should have a voice.

Reflection

Three ways I relate to this chapter

1. _____
_____
_____
_____
_____

2. _____
_____
_____
_____
_____

3. _____
_____
_____
_____
_____

If I am honest with myself – this is my situation

My situation (trauma, PTSD, abuse) is negatively impacting
my life in the following way/s

_____

_____

_____

_____

_____

_____

_____

_____

_____

_____

_____

_____

_____

_____

_____

_____

_____

_____

_____

_____

To move on to a healthy recovey I need to

_____

_____

_____

_____

_____

_____

_____

_____

_____

_____

_____

_____

_____

_____

_____

_____

_____

_____

_____

_____

Steps/goals to help move forward

1. _____

_____

_____

_____

_____

_____

_____

2. _____

_____

_____

_____

_____

_____

_____

3. _____

_____

_____

_____

_____

_____

_____

Helpful Resources

Good Therapy
https://www.goodtherapy.org
Good Therapy: Complex PTSD: Response to Prolonged Trauma

Parent Teacher Association
https://www.pta.org
For Families- Healthy Minds- Programs

Harvard Health
Health Information and Medical Information
www.Helpguide.org

Substance Abuse and Mental Health Service Admin
https://www.samhsa.gov/find-help/national-helpline
https://www.samhsa.gov/talk-they-hear-you/parent-resources
https://www.samhsa.gov/mental-health
https://www.samhsa.gov/find-support/how-to-cope
https://findtreatment.gov

988 Suicide & Crisis Lifeline
Free and confidential support for people in distress, 24/7

THE WISEST OWL WATCHED FROM ABOVE
ONLY TO LEARN FROM BELOW

About the Authors

SHERRI JOST lives in Wentzville, MO with her two daughters and two dogs. She is currently working on her Ph.D. in Health Administration and is writing her dissertation in mental health. Her personal experiences, education, and life events have brought her to this point in her life. She believes her story can help change lives for the better, and support people who are challenged with trauma, abuse, and PTSD, while also providing valuable resources and testimonies. According to Ms. Jost, each person is unique, no two people walk the same path, and every story matters. The road is hard, life is a battlefield, and survival is the key!

About the Authors

TINA CLARIN (nee Trebilcock) is originally from Minnesota and currently lives in Arizona with her husband, son, and 2 dog. She is a mother of four and grandmother of two. She has earned three Master's degrees in the fields of Education, Psychology, and Innovative Leadership. She is currently completing her Doctor of Philosophy in General Psychology: Cognition and Instruction. Ms. Clarin is the Owner and Director of an Early Education Learning Center and is also adjunct faculty for two local universities. Ms. Clarin's personal and professional experiences with children and adults with trauma, PTSD, ADD/ADHD, Bi-Polar, Borderline Personality Disorder (BPD) and other mental health concerns has given her a unique perspective on parenting, self-care, and finding resources to help people effectively and positively navigate their situation and have successful lives.

References

Appleyard, K., & Osofsky, J. D. (2003). Parenting after trauma: Supporting parents and caregivers in the treatment of children impacted by violence. Infant Mental Health Journal: Official Publication of The World Association for Infant Mental Health, 24(2), 111-125

Geller, J. L. (2006). A History of Private Psychiatric Hospitals in the USA: From Start to Almost Finished. Psychiatric Quarterly, 77(1), 1-41. doi: 10.1007/s11126-006-7959-5 (As posted on the Rochester Center of Behavioral Medicine.net website)

Ryder, G. (Nov 30, 2021). 6 Ways to Help Someone with PTSD. https://psychcentral.com/ptsd/how-to-help-someone-with-ptsd

Ryder, G. (Jan 4, 2022). What Is Trauma? https://psychcentral.com/health/what-is-trauma

Shalaby, R. A. H., & Agyapong, V. I. O. (2020). Peer Support in Mental Health: Literature Review. JMIR mental health, 7(6), e15572. https://doi.org/10.2196/15572

Van der Kolk B. (2000). Posttraumatic stress disorder and the nature of trauma. Dialogues in clinical neuroscience, 2(1), 7–22. https://doi.org/10.31887/DCNS.2000.2.1/bvdkolk

Wilcoxon, L. A., Meiser-Stedman, R., & Burgess, A. (2021). Posttraumatic stress disorder in parents following their child's single-event trauma: A meta-analysis of prevalence rates and risk factor correlates. Clinical child and family psychology review, 1-19

www.ingramcontent.com/pod-product-compliance
Lightning Source LLC
Chambersburg PA
CBHW070057100426

42740CB00013B/2861